ONE DIRECTION

Here We Go

Publisher and Creative Director: Nick Wells
Project Editor & Picture Research: Polly Prior
Art Director and Layout Design: Mike Spender
Digital Design and Production: Chris Herbert

Special thanks to: Emma Chafer, Esme Chapman, Jane Donovan, Stephen Feather, Dawn Laker

FLAME TREE PUBLISHING

Crabtree Hall, Crabtree Lane
Fulham, London SW6 6TY
United Kingdom

www.flametreepublishing.com

First published 2012

12 14 16 15 13
1 3 5 7 9 10 8 6 4 2

A CIP record for this book is available from the British Library upon request.

ISBN 978-0-85775-888-0

Printed in China

ONE DIRECTION

Here We Go

NADIA COHEN

FOREWORD: MANGO SAUL, EDITOR, SUGARSCAPE.COM

FLAME TREE
PUBLISHING

Contents

Foreword

Simon Cowell could see One Direction coming a mile off. Five young, good-looking chaps with reasonable singing voices and charm that would make any girl fall for them. TA DA! 1D were formed, as if by magic. The *X Factor* guru knew exactly what he was creating when he brought together Zayn Malik, Niall Horan, Louis Tomlinson, Liam Payne and Harry Styles – a boy band that were going to make him a ton of cash by selling millions of records. Globally.

Having the fastest-selling album of 2011 is a mean accomplishment. Being the first UK group to ever bag a No. 1 in the US *Billboard 200* is achieving the almost-impossible. Not even six-album Take That have mastered the US charts like One Direction have in just two. Actually, we need to forget Take That and any other boy band you can think of: we've not seen a pop phenomenon like One Direction since The Beatles and Beatlemania.

Some people may think that putting One Direction in the same sentence as The Beatles is complete madness, especially since the *X Factor* not-even-runners-up have only released two albums and a handful of singles. It's not madness. The band has charisma, good song writers behind them and, more importantly, Simon Cowell and his company Syco orchestrating the perfect pop machine.

If anyone thinks what One Direction have achieved so far is utterly amazing, we haven't seen anything yet. There's plenty more to come from this fresh new quintet...

Mango Saul

Editor, Sugarscape.com

New British Invasion

In September 2010, the world had never heard of **Harry Styles**, **Niall Horan**, **Liam Payne**, **Zayn Malik** and **Louis Tomlinson**. The five boys did not even know each other's names and yet, within just 18 months of meeting each other, the singers – who joined forces to create the global phenomenon that is One Direction – had made history.

And on 21 March 2012, they became the first-ever UK group to debut at No. 1 on the American *Billboard* chart with their album, *Up All Night*. Previously, the highest entry for a UK group's debut was when the Spice Girls unleashed *Spice* in 1997; they had cracked America in style.

When One Direction heard about their record-breaking moment, they were in the middle of a jam-packed promotional tour across the States, causing pandemonium to break out wherever they went, as thousands of love-struck fans turned out for a glimpse of the biggest British group since The Beatles landed, almost 50 years earlier.

The Original Invasion

In December 1963, the CBS *Evening News* with Walter Cronkite ran a story on American TV about a new band called The Beatles, who were proving hugely popular in the UK, and played their hit single, 'She Loves You'. But what was intended to be a light-hearted news item sparked a frenzy across the

'We've got a *lot of big dreams*. We want to have *No. 1s, travel* a lot, go back to *America* and have as *much fun* as possible – *I don't* think that's *too much* to ask!'

Harry Styles

nation: radio stations and record stores were flooded with requests for a record they did not have in stock, and when a DJ in Washington DC played 'I Want To Hold Your Hand', The Beatles' label, Parlophone, had no choice but to quickly release the record in the States – by then in the grip of a phenomenon which would become known as 'Beatlemania'.

'I Want To Hold Your Hand' reached No. 1 on the *Billboard* chart in January 1964, and when The Beatles appeared on *The Ed Sullivan Show* on 9 February, their position in pop history was secured. Forty-five per cent of Americans watched their now-iconic performance and, within weeks, Paul McCartney, John Lennon, George Harrison and Ringo Starr held the top-five positions on the chart – the only time any group has ever achieved that feat. The group's massive success continued on both sides of the Atlantic until they eventually broke up in 1970 due to internal tensions.

Making It Happen

Before they even set foot on American soil, One Direction were already superstars, thanks to clever use of social media. Executives from their label, Columbia Records, decided to use Facebook and Twitter for their marketing campaign instead of the usual strategy of releasing a single on the radio. Taking a gamble, co-chairman Steve Barnett decided to mount a four-month, word-of-mouth campaign with the intention of building a fan base before a single was ever

released or even played on the radio in America. Columbia asked fans to sign petitions and enter video competitions to win a concert in their hometown.

The gamble paid off spectacularly well and, within a few weeks, One Direction's Facebook page had 400,000 followers in the States. Their single 'What Makes You Beautiful' sold more than 131,000 copies, although it had yet to be played on the radio. In fact, radio stations were flooded with calls from fans demanding to hear their songs before the boys had even left London.

'It feels so strange when I look back to before The X Factor, when I didn't even have a passport and hadn't been outside the U.K. Now all of a sudden I've been to all of these amazing places.'

Zayn Malik

Pandemonium Breaks Out!

One Direction's very first appearance on Canadian television in March 2010 was intended to test the water on the other side of the Atlantic. But few could have predicted the overwhelming reception the boys would receive. Officials were forced to shut down the streets surrounding the Toronto headquarters of Much Music when word got out that the band would be showing up. Thousands of screaming fans lined the streets behind the barriers and that was just the beginning. When they made their American TV debut on the *Today* show at the Rockefeller Center in New York City, 15,000 people mobbed the place. A few weeks later, more than a dozen hysterical Australian fans required first aid after passing out as the band were interviewed on Channel 7's *Sunrise* show in Sydney's central business district. The boys had also been due to perform a gig for Austereo radio station but the location was changed at the very last minute amid grave security concerns.

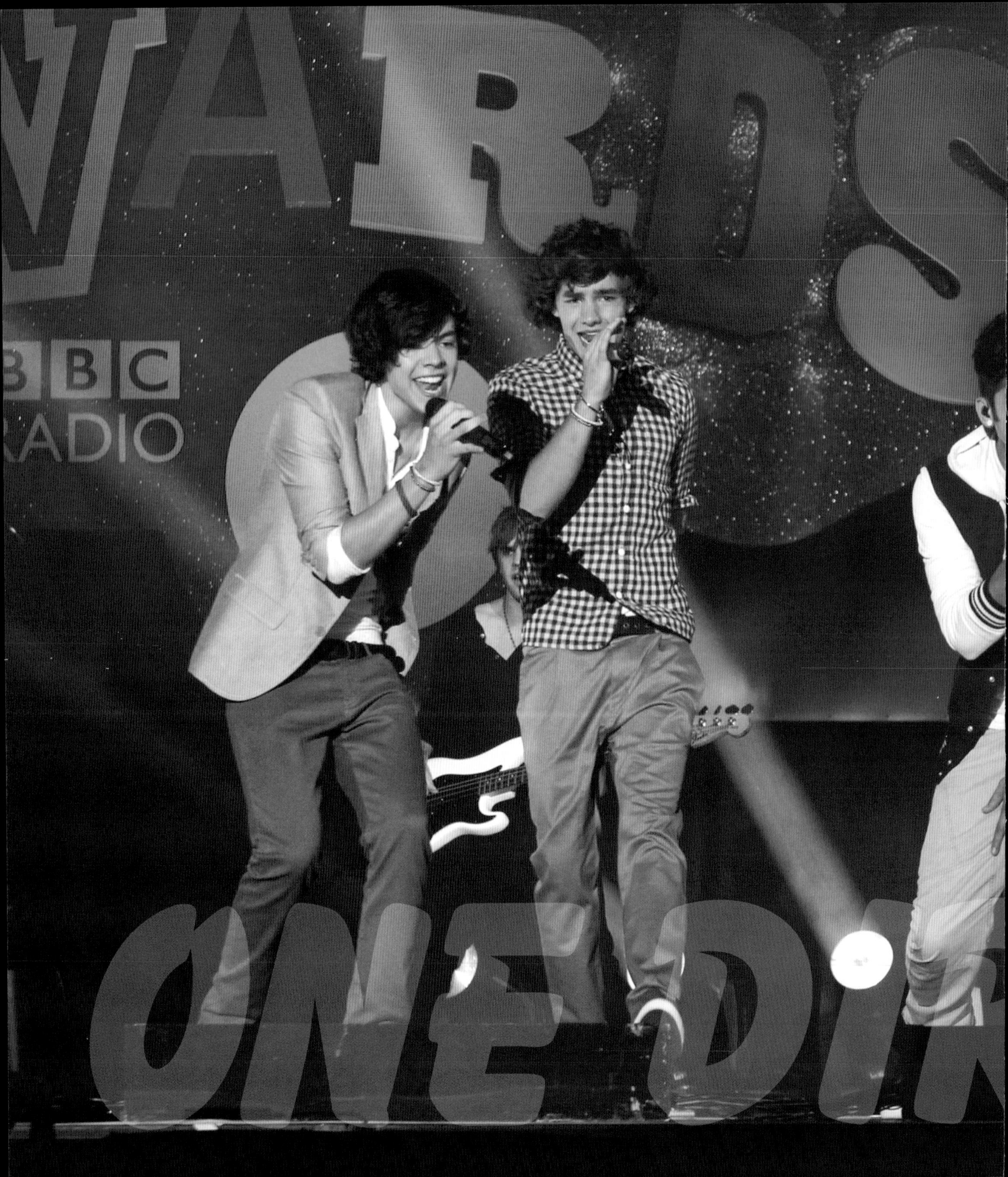
BBC
RADIO
ONE DIR

The Boys Are Back In Town

Back home in the UK, there is just as much excitement about the band's success, with cameras and love-struck admirers following their every move. Not content with chart success, the boys also have their sights set on the big screen, with a road movie, *One Direction – A Year In The Making*, charting their rise to stardom. Comedian James Corden's TV production company Fulwell 73 secured the rights to make the film and One Direction's creator Simon Cowell agreed to stump up half of the £150,000 cost. Simon explained: 'You're going to see an explosion here, the likes of which we haven't seen since Take That – and I think that's exciting!'

As well as their high-profile performances around the world, the movie will also catch them showing their youthful side, with pranks such as a cake fight at Manchester's G-A-Y nightclub on Niall's 18th birthday. Harry confirmed the rumours of an eagerly anticipated film about their lives, revealing that a number of companies were interested in the project.

Online Sensation

They may have only come third on *The X Factor* (2010), but Simon Cowell spotted their potential and the boys were immediately signed to his record label, Syco. Syco's managing director Sonny Takhar believes their runaway success is all down to the power of social media. 'It's a real moment,' he says. 'Social media has become the new radio –

'People think that a *boy band* is air-grabs and being *dressed* in all one *colour*. We're *boys* in a *band* – we're trying to do *something different* from what *people* would think is the *typical* kind of *boy band*. We're trying to do *different* kinds of *music* and we're just trying to be *ourselves*, not *squeaky clean*.'

Niall Horan

it's never broken an act globally like this before.' The boys have millions of 'likes' on Facebook, with the number increasing daily and, according to statistics from Google, 3.35 million search for One Direction-related pages every month. Although each of the boys has their own Twitter account, which they update several times a day, the band's management also employs a social media team to keep up with the relentless demand from fans responding to the boys' every word.

'Louis put on Twitter the other day that he wanted some Curiously Cinnamon cereal – and someone brought some to the hotel – it's amazing!'

Liam Payne

Twitter Followers

All the boys tweet regularly to help them stay close to their fans and each has millions of followers on Twitter. They make sure they update fans on their movements and feelings. Unfortunately, this can have its downside too, as the girls

who have been romantically linked to a member of the group have all suffered vicious online abuse and bullying from jealous fans. On the other hand, dreams really do come true for some fans! Receptionist Anna Crotti caught Zayn's eye when the guys visited Nova FM in Sydney, where she worked, and he ended up asking her on a date!

The Image

Within days of their first appearance on TV, each of the boys had become known for a particular feature. Niall is now 'the cute little Irish one', Zayn is 'the quiet and mysterious one', Liam is 'the sensible one', Harry is 'the charming one' and Louis is 'the funny one'. Luckily, the lads do not seem to mind the labels but Niall is determined they should not be seen as being the same as all the other boy bands around.

'We'd had a lot of *experience*, so we didn't *freeze* in front of the cameras – we were *just* ourselves. When you're used to it, you soon *forget* that the cameras are there.' Zayn Malik

'Some days I read 100 great Twitter comments and there *may* be one from someone saying they *don't* like me. If I'm having a bad day for some reason, that's the one I remember and it can make me feel a bit down. Then I'll go back and read the nice messages again and they'll lift me – they mean a lot to all of us.'

Harry Styles

Getting Together

'When the *day* of the *audition* finally *arrived*, I decided I *didn't* want to go. I was *lying* in *bed*, *refusing* to get up, and it was my *mum* who told me *I had to* and made me get out the *door!*'

Zayn Malik

The boys all auditioned as individual contestants on the seventh series of ITV1's talent show *The X Factor* in 2010 and that was the moment when everything in their lives was changed for ever. That year, Simon Cowell was the mentor for the groups and declared himself 'genuinely very excited' about One Direction, who quickly became his best hope of winning the competition. Their performances provoked such loud screams from the studio audience that the judges' comments could hardly be heard. Amid all the hysteria, Simon confidently predicted his group were going to win: 'They get on well and they have steel in their eyes, and that's what I look for in my artists,' he noted. 'I think they'll go far.'

'The *best* moment for *me* out of the whole thing was when we were *told* we were going to be put in a *band together*, but I never for a *moment* thought that *things* would end up *like this*.'

Harry Styles

The boys themselves were not completely confident of winning, but hoped to follow in the footsteps of JLS, who went on to build huge success from being *X Factor* runners-up in 2008. JLS's first single 'Beat Again' was a No. 1 hit in July 2009, and four months later their album *JLS* also debuted in the top spot. A headline tour and a BRIT Award swiftly followed, before another two bestselling albums, *Outta This World* (2010) and *Jukebox* (2011). Every time the JLS boys make a public appearance they are mobbed by legions of teenage fans – and have even complained about the girls' mothers making passes at them!

Auditioning Alone

Harry was already playing in a band called White Eskimo with some school friends when his mother Anne filled out *The X Factor* application form because he was too nervous. Liam had endured the audition process before, having first tried out when he was just 14, but only made it as far as the Judges' Houses stage that year. Louis also made a previous attempt in 2009, but didn't even make it through the first round. However, his rendition of 'Make You Feel My Love' (originally a Bob Dylan number, and later hugely successful for Adele) impressed the panel the following year. Niall prepared for his audition with a local *Stars In Their Eyes* show, where he was compared to Justin Bieber. Zayn was persuaded to give the show a try by his music teacher, Mrs Fox, who had already cast him in lead roles in several school productions, but he almost did not go through with it.

'To be *thrown* together like that and have to get to know *each other* was a bit *scary*. We're all quite *different* as well, so we *did bicker* occasionally. We get on *brilliantly* now, though. As soon as we were *honest* with *each other* it worked, and we've *ended up* being really *close mates*.'

Liam Payne

Meeting The Boys

All the boys did well at their individual auditions and made it through to the next stage – known as 'Boot Camp'. However, the competition in the boys' category was fierce and none of them was selected to move on to Judges' Houses until guest judge Nicole Scherzinger half-jokingly suggested they perform together, which would allow them to qualify for the groups category. They had only minutes to decide their future and choose a band name they would be stuck with.

Forming A Band

To prepare for the Judges' Houses stage of the competition at Simon Cowell's luxurious 20-bedroom villa in Marbella in Spain, the boys all went to stay with Harry's stepfather Robin in Cheshire and it was there that they started to form a bond. Of course they sailed through to the live shows and after the elimination of the other groups – F.Y.D., Diva Fever and Belle Amie – within four weeks, made it through to the final, in December 2010. They finished in third place, behind runner-up Rebecca Ferguson and the overall winner, Matt Cardle. Immediately after the final show, 'Forever Young' (the song they would have released, had they won) was leaked on to the internet and caused a sensation that would dramatically change five young lives for ever.

'We *played* a lot of *gigs* once the *series finished* and it was all *new* for me — *I'd never even been to a* *nightclub* before. *I lived* a very *quiet, boring* and *sheltered life* before the band, so *absolutely* *everything that happened was* a *learning curve.*'

Zayn Malik

Making Waves

When *The X Factor* final was over, the boys were devastated at missing out on the top prize and were all in tears until Simon Cowell called his favourite group into his dressing room, backstage at the Fountain Studios in Wembley, and made an announcement. 'You were great on the show,' he told them. 'Sony are going to sign you up in the morning. You're going to be all right, don't worry about coming third,' he added, before giving them all a hug, but urging them to keep the news secret until after Christmas.

In January 2011, One Direction signed a £2m record contract with Simon's company Syco before heading off to LA for five days to record some early tracks in the first professional recording studio any of them had ever seen. But there was no time to complete an album, for they were contractually obliged to spend the next three months on the X Factor Live Tour. The UK tour, which kicked off in February at the LG Arena in Birmingham, was a triumph.

X Factor Live Tour

The first time the boys hit the road together was alongside the other finalists from the show, travelling across Britain to perform to sell-out crowds. For One Direction, it was a taste of things to come as they were greeted by hordes of screaming girls at every venue. During the tour, the boys really started to forge strong friendships, carve out their image and along the way they gained a reputation for being pranksters, wrecking dressing rooms in Sheffield and Liverpool with messy food fights!

'We were completely *mobbed*. I was wearing a *hoodie* and *half* of it got *ripped* off me. Later, when we went to a *book signing*, there was a *girl* who had brought the *sleeve* along to *show me* – and even *asked* me to *sign it*! I thought it was *hilarious*.'

Louis Tomlinson

What Makes You Beautiful

When One Direction released their debut single on 11 September 2011, it broke the pre-order sales record for Sony Music. A week later, 'What Makes You Beautiful' stormed into the UK Singles Chart at No. 1, having sold 153,965 copies – the highest first-week sales for any song that year. It would remain at No. 1 in the UK and Ireland for four weeks. Days later, One Direction announced their debut UK dates and tickets for the Up All Night Tour were sold out within minutes of being released.

When the single was released in America in February 2012, it debuted on the *Billboard* Hot 100, going on to peak at No. 4 for two weeks.

'It was **nerve-wracking**, trying to find the **first single**, because of course we wanted it to be **perfect**. We **all** got to do a lot of **co-writing**, which was really **important** for **us** and we loved being **involved**.' *Liam Payne*

Debut Album

One Direction released their first album *Up All Night* in November 2011, having developed it with producer Saran Pyrotechny in Sweden. It included collaborations with major stars, including Kelly Clarkson and Ed Sheeran, and was to prove a huge hit, following their relentless promotional schedule which included performances on popular television shows including ITV1's *Red or Black?*, BBC *Children In Need*, *BBC Radio 1 Teen Awards*, the *Jingle Bell Ball* at the O2 Arena in London and an appearance on the final of the eighth series of *The X Factor*.

'Our **aim** with the **album** was to recreate the **boy band sound**, do something no one else is doing at the **moment**. We wanted some **big songs** that would surprise people; we wanted to be part of the **writing process**. We said from the **word go** that we wanted to be really involved, and we were **very lucky** that we got the **chance**.'

Niall Horan

Niall

Niall James Horan was born on 13 September 1993 in the small town of Mullingar, Ireland. Following his parents' divorce when he was five, Niall and his brother Greg split their time between the homes of their mother Maura Gallagher and dad Bobby Horan, before eventually deciding to live with Bobby when Maura remarried in 2005. Niall explained: 'I ended up moving in with my dad because he lived in town, so I had more friends there and it was more convenient for school and other stuff.' Although small for his age, Niall was a popular pupil at Colatitude Muire, a school for boys founded by the Christian Brothers. Although he did not excel academically, teachers recall that he was good at French and showed great potential.

'The *simple fact* is that I *spent* too much time *messing* about. I thought *school* was all about having a *craic* and *acting* like a *fool.*'

Niall Horan

'I'm 16 and I want to be a big name like *Beyoncé* and *Justin Bieber*. I've been compared to him a few times and it's not a bad comparison. I want to sell out arenas, make an album and work with some of the best artists in the world.'

Niall Horan, to X Factor judges at his audition

Musical Beginnings

Niall was into music from a very young age; at six years old, he started to play the recorder and took up the guitar aged 12. 'I was always the kid that picked up the nearest instrument and just loved music,' he recalls. His family first spotted his vocal talent when he was singing in the back of the car. 'My auntie said she thought the radio was on. Exactly the same thing happened to Michael Bublé with his dad – he's my absolute hero so I like the fact we have a similar story. My auntie said she always knew I'd be famous from then on, but I never thought anything of it.'

Before his big break, Niall was chosen as a support act for a previous *X Factor* contestant, Lloyd Daniels, when he performed in Dublin and was brimming with confidence when he himself auditioned for the show soon afterwards.

The Girls

Niall had his first girlfriend at school, but the romance fizzled out after just a few months and he has been pretty much single ever since, although he knows what he is looking for: 'I like the natural look and someone who can take a bit of banter, have a laugh, and who likes the same things as me – if you go out with me, you have to want to come to a football match. I support Derby County, and I always have.'

Niall was said to be dating *X Factor* finalist Amelia Lily in 2011, but that has not stopped armies of admirers from trying their luck, although he admits to feeling overwhelmed by pushy crowds. Indeed he panicked the first time the boys were mobbed at Heathrow Airport shortly after *The X Factor* finished.

'I'm really claustrophobic, so I was panicking a bit when we had to run through everyone and hide. I was so relieved when a police riot van came and got us – I still can't believe it happened, it feels like it was all some kind of mad dream.'

Niall Horan

Heroes

Niall often says the best thing about being a star is having the chance to meet some of his favourite performers. He says Ed

Sheeran is a major influence, so when he collaborated with the boys on the song 'Moments' for their debut album, Niall was honoured and a little starstruck!

Niall made Michael Bublé laugh by telling him: 'I spent £200 on tickets for your concert in Dublin and I had to give them up because of *X Factor*.' Although the singer offered him tickets for any show he wanted, Niall cheekily replied: 'No, Michael – I just want my £200 back!'

'I was always into *pop music* when I was really *young*. I really liked *Westlife*, so to get to meet them and have a *chat* and a *craic* was *brilliant*. They were just *laid-back* and down to *earth* – must be an *Irish thing*.'

Niall Horan

'It's *amazing* how *word spreads* about where *we* are. We do have to be *a bit more careful* because even if we just *pop out* to get something and people *recognize us*, it can go a *bit crazy*.'

Niall Horan

Zayn

Yaser and Tricia Malik were thrilled with the arrival of little Zayn Javadd on 12 January 1993. He grew up with three sisters in Bradford, where he attended Tong High School, and turned out to be rather a handful. 'I was quite hyperactive,' he recalled. 'I'd be bouncing off the walls and jumping from one room to the next. Even in the house, my mum used to put me in my pram because I was so full-on.'

But Zayn was a bright kid and by the age of eight he had a reading age of 18, as well as a talent for art and drama. He joined the school choir and was cast in productions of *Grease*, *Arabian Nights* and *Bugsy Malone*. Although he says he still feels like that kid from Bradford, Zayn is now recognized everywhere he goes and finds that difficult to deal with. 'I worry about being seen as a bad person,' he admits. 'Everyone makes mistakes, but when you're famous it's plastered everywhere. I want to be open, but I'm still learning about how open I can be and who I can trust totally.'

The Girls

Zayn credits the female influence of his three sisters Doniya, Waliyha and Safaa for making him good with girls: 'I was much more sensitive when I was growing up because I was around women all the time. I also think as a result I understand women more than the average man does,

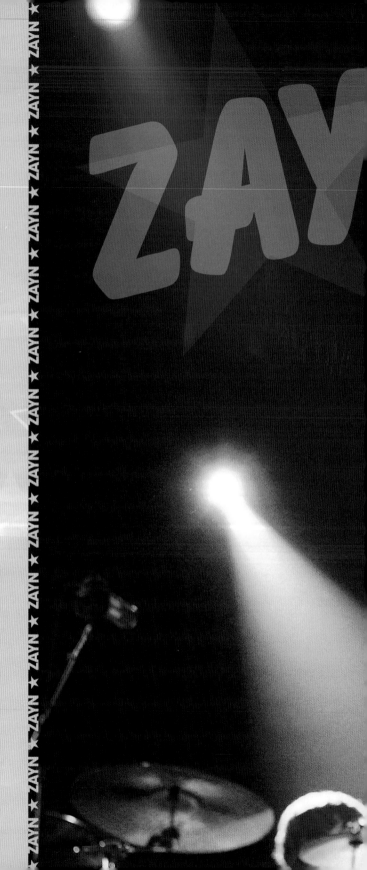

to be honest.' After his first kiss at the age of 12, Zayn had his first real girlfriend when he was 15 and they were together for nine months. Since then, he claims, he's only had 'two or three proper girlfriends.'

Zayn dated fellow *X Factor* contestant Rebecca Ferguson during their stint on the competition, causing controversy due to the six-year age difference, but the romance fizzled out after just four months. He was also linked to singer Cher Lloyd, Belle Amie's Geneva Lane and most recently, he has been dating Little Mix star Perrie Edwards, although initially they denied their budding romance. 'I wouldn't say I've got a specific type looks-wise when it comes to girls,' he says. 'I want someone who I feel comfortable around and I can spoil a bit; someone I can get on with. I've become a lot less shallow as I've got older and personality is very important to me now.'

'I absolutely *loved being* on *stage* and becoming *somebody else*. I found being a *character* really *liberating* and I used to get such a *rush* from *acting*.'

Zayn Malik

'Someone can be the *best looking* in the *world*, but if they're *boring* there's nothing *worse* – you have to have *something* to *stimulate* you *mentally*.' Zayn Malik

> '*A year ago*, the thought of being on *stage* in front of that many *people* would have been enough to make me *physically sick*, but now *I go out* and *walk* around the *stage* and *I feel so much* more *confident*.'
>
> *Zayn Malik*

The Rebel

The only member of the band who smokes, Zayn also has ten tattoos including a Yin Yang Tai-Chi symbol on his wrist, the word 'ZAP!' on his forearm, his grandfather's name 'Walter' in Arabic on his chest, a 'born lucky' symbol on his stomach, a silver fern on his neck and an inscription across his collarbone that says 'be true to who you are' in Arabic.

Although he is close to the other lads, Zayn admits that from time to time, he gets frustrated with their pranks and untidiness: 'Having time alone is how I keep myself sane,' he says. And while he appears to have the world at his feet, Zayn suffers such bad stage fright that at one point during *The X Factor* he refused to go on stage to dance. In fact, Simon Cowell had to personally beg him to join the others as they learnt a basic routine. Zayn says: 'My confidence has improved so much since Boot Camp and I can have much more of a laugh with the boys about it all.'

In January 2012 he vowed to kick his cigarette habit, saying 'My New Year's resolution is definitely to quit smoking. I need to do it.' Although numerous Facebook pages were created to encourage the singer to quit, they have, so far, been in vain.

Liam

Liam James Payne gave his parents, Karen and Geoff, quite a scare when he was born three weeks early on 29 August 1993 and needed resuscitation. As a result, one of his kidneys was scarred and dysfunctional. As a child, he endured 32 injections in his arm every morning and evening to cope with the pain. Now one kidney does not work and so he has to be careful not to drink too much – even water – and to stay healthy.

At school, Liam was something of an entrepreneur, buying boxes of sweets and selling them on for a profit, making himself around £50 a week. Although a sporty kid, he was bullied at school and took up boxing to learn how to fight back. 'I needed to find a way to defend myself,' he explains. 'I was, at 12 years old, fighting the 38-year-old trainer. I broke my nose, had a perforated eardrum and I was always coming home with a bruised, puffy face, but it gave me confidence. I got pretty good over the next couple of years.'

Musical Beginnings

As a child, Liam was always singing karaoke and joined the school choir when he was nine. He even won a solo, aged 13, when his choir joined with other schools to set a new world record for the number of people singing in unison. His mother Karen would juggle shifts as a nursery

> *'It was **horrible** to be **turned away**, but if I had made the **live shows** I wouldn't have known what **hit me** – I would have been **gone** straight away.'*
>
> Liam Payne

> *'My **mates** used to **wind me up** and pretend that **girls** liked me when they didn't, so I'd **ask** them out and they'd say **no**, which was **mortifying**.'*
>
> Liam Payne

nurse to accompany him on all his auditions and was by his side the first time he auditioned for *The X Factor* at the age of 14, wearing a pair of borrowed jeans (Armani, from his sister's boyfriend) and shoes with a hole in them (just old). He later explained: 'I didn't really have much of an interest in fashion generally, so when my first *X Factor* audition came around I had absolutely nothing nice to wear.' Liam waited nine hours to do the audition and eventually made it through to Judges' Houses, but Simon told him that he was not ready for the competition and asked him to come back in two years.

When he was 16, by then studying music technology at City of Wolverhampton College, Liam decided to give the show another try. 'I was the only one of the lads who really had to think about whether or not it was a good idea to become a band. I'd been working as a solo artist for so long that I couldn't imagine not doing that, but as soon as I made the decision to go for it, I knew I had done the right thing,' he explained.

The Girls

Although he landed his first girlfriend at the age of five, Liam did not always have such success with the ladies. A few years later, he asked the same girl out 22 times and she only agreed to go on a date after he sang to her! His audition song, 'Cry Me A River', was aimed at a girl who cheated on him.

When Liam started out in the show, he was dating his childhood sweetheart, Shannon Murphy, but their relationship fizzled out due to the amount of time spent apart while on *The X Factor*. 'We had to be apart for months on end so it put a lot of pressure on the relationship and we finally split up,' he admits. He dated Danielle Peazer, a backing dancer for The Saturdays and Jessie J, for two years, after meeting her on the show in 2010.

Danielle resisted Liam's charms at first because she felt he was too young for her, but eventually he convinced her to let him take her on a date. She was a good influence on him, encouraging him to clean up his act after they started sharing a flat. They even got themselves a dog, Loki, but eventually agreed to go their separate ways in 2013, saying that their hectic schedules did not leave them enough time for a proper relationship, but they remain the best of friends.

The Sensible One

While the other boys tend to party pretty hard after coming off stage on a high, Liam admits that he prefers time to himself: 'I'm a fairly quiet person so I used to go to my room to be by myself. I've got a lot I want to achieve so drinking doesn't interest me.' Because of his kidney problems, Liam watches his diet carefully, particularly the amount of salt and protein he consumes, and prefers to unwind by working out in the gym. As a result, he has impressive six-pack abs to show for it and is happy to be known as the 'dad' of the group.

'I think even when I'm old enough to drink, I won't. My plan is to learn to drive so I can ferry the other lads around and act as security when we go out.'

Liam Payne

Harry

1 February 1994 was the day when the world welcomed Harry Edward Styles to his family home in Holmes Chapel, Cheshire. His parents, Anne Cox and Des Styles, divorced when Harry was seven and they moved into the pub, run by Anne. 'That was quite a weird time,' recalled Harry. 'I remember crying about it. I didn't really get what was going on properly, I was just sad that my parents wouldn't be together any more.' He and his older sister Gemma were delighted when, five years later, their mother married Robin Twist.

At school, Harry was a keen badminton player, thanks to his father's enthusiasm for the sport: 'I liked the fact that it wasn't the most obvious sport to get into, and that you need quite a lot of skill to play it,' he says.

Musical Beginnings

Ever since he was at nursery school, Harry has loved performing to an audience and has appeared in productions of *Chitty Chitty Bang Bang* and *Barney*. He was also a keen singer and, when his grandfather, Harold, gave him a karaoke machine, he learnt all the words to dozens of Elvis Presley songs.

Harry was delighted when in 2006 he was asked to become the lead singer with a local band called White Eskimo.

Together with lead guitarist Haydn Morris, bass guitarist Nick Clough and drummer Will Sweeny, they won a Battle of the Bands competition. Following their success, they were asked to perform at a friend's wedding and were spotted by a music producer, who told Harry he reminded him of Mick Jagger.

'He's a mummy's boy – sometimes he phones up to five times a day.'

Anne Cox (Harry's mother)

The Looks

Harry is famous for his carefully coiffed hair and admits he has always taken pride in his much-admired appearance: 'My hair has changed a lot over the years,' he says. 'The worst thing was probably when I had blond streaks put in it when I was about eight. I thought it was cool when I went into school the day after having it done but looking back, I looked like a douche.'

Perhaps it helps that he is a big fan of naturism and was filmed naked several times while in *The X Factor* house.

'Now we were serious about carrying the band on and trying to get a deal one day. Being in front of an audience with the band had given me a taste for performing and I wanted to do more and more.'

Harry Styles

'Stripping off is very liberating,' he explains. 'I feel so free. It's always a spur-of-the-moment thing, but no one seemed to mind. I became a lot more confident during my time in the show and my confidence came out in my nakedness – I think you could safely say I'm not shy.'

Harry's good looks have made him hugely popular around the globe and the band's US management are trying to make him into the lead singer, but despite the adoration, he does his best to stay grounded.

*'It was a **new experience** for us all because it was like living in a **student flat**. We were just **messing** around, but it was a **really good** way of getting to know each other's **personalities**. We were learning **little bits** about each other by having **silly banter**.'*

Harry Styles

The Girls

Harry has a reputation for being quite a ladies' man and, unsurprisingly, was popular with the opposite sex from an early age: 'I wasn't one of those boys who thought girls were smelly and didn't like them,' he laughs. He dated several lucky girls at school, including Abi – who he describes as his first serious girlfriend. During the show, Harry sparked widespread controversy by dating presenter Caroline Flack, who was 15 years older than him. Harry and Caroline ended their three-month romance in January 2012, shortly before the band left for their tour of America and Australia.

He has since been linked to others, including Emma Ostilly, Emily Atack and, more recently, pop princess Taylor Swift. Their month-long romance came to an end as 2013 began, and will no doubt provide Taylor with rich songwriting material.

Harry adores his fans, and often takes them treats when he knows they have been waiting hours for a glimpse of him. He said: 'Some fans came to my house over Christmas, but I felt terrible that they were standing in the freezing cold because of me. We'll never complain about people coming to see us or wanting autographs or photos.'

'With some *girls* I may not find them *attractive* immediately, but then I *really* get to like them because their *personality* is *so attractive*. I like someone I can have a *conversation* with and I would *always* look for *someone* who could get on with *my parents* – it's *important* to *me* that my *family* like her *too*.'

Harry Styles

'I would *never want* to get *bigheaded* – it's such an *unattractive trait* and I can't imagine *myself* ever being like that. I *always* want to be aware of staying *true* to *myself*.'

Harry Styles

Louis

On Christmas Eve 1991, Louis William Tomlinson arrived, and since his parents, Johannah and Troy, split up when he was tiny, he took his stepfather Mark's surname. He has four younger stepsisters: Charlotte, Félicité and twins Daisy and Phoebe. As a child, he planned to become an actor and after finding himself an agent, he won small parts in the TV shows *Fat Friends*, *If I Had You* and *Waterloo Road*.

Louis attended acting school in Barnsley, South Yorkshire, but he was too busy having fun, filming and appearing in local plays, so ended up failing his first year of A-levels, following which he moved to a local comprehensive. He was always a hard worker and landed himself part-time jobs at Toys R Us and his local football stadium and cinema, but ended up being fired from the cinema after he failed to turn up for a shift because he was at his *X Factor* audition.

'Acting is something I would definitely think about pursuing later on, but for now it's all about the band.'

Louis Tomlinson

Musical Beginnings

At the age of 14, Louis joined a band called The Rogue, who had been looking for a singer. Alongside his friends, Geoff, Jona, Jamie and Stan, he performed for his class and gradually built up his confidence. At school, he landed the lead role in a production of *Grease*, which he looks back on with pride: 'I still get emotional when I watch the video because it was such a special time,' he says. 'I will never forget it.'

Louis was always a huge fan of Robbie Williams, and when Williams agreed to sing a duet of his hit 'She's The One' with the group for the live final of *The X Factor* in December 2010, all the lads agreed that working with the star was one of the highlights of the entire show. Louis says that Michael Jackson was also 'a real inspiration.'

The Girls

Louis has always had an easy way with girls, thanks to his sisters. 'When I was growing up, there were five women running around so I suppose in some ways it did teach me about women,' he explains. 'I'm certainly not intimidated by them because I'm so used to them!'

His first proper girlfriend was Hannah Walker, a primary school teacher from Doncaster, who made regular visits to London to support him during *The X Factor*. Two months after they split, he started dating politics student and part-time model,

'I really *enjoyed performing* and yet *I never* had the *courage* to do a whole school *assembly* because I was so *intimidated*. It's so *weird* to think that I've ended up *performing* in front of *thousands!*'

Louis Tomlinson

Eleanor Calder. Hannah said later: 'When I look at him on the television now I know him as two different people – one is the boy from Doncaster, and the other is Louis from One Direction.'

These days he is smitten with Eleanor and is already thinking about starting a family.

'I absolutely love babies and kids. The boys are always taking the mickey out of me for how broody I am. I definitely, definitely want kids of my own one day.'

Louis Tomlinson

The Pranks

Louis first gained a reputation for being the prankster of the group when he left *The X Factor* studios wearing a hospital gown. When the boys were on the X Factor Live Tour in February 2012, he landed himself in trouble for wrecking dressing rooms: while in Sheffield, Louis tried to throw an apple core into the bin,

but missed, which resulted in everyone throwing apples at the wall. A few days later, they did the same in Liverpool, but got away with it because they hid all the fruit in the shower and shut the curtains! Louis also infuriated fellow contestant Wagner by covering him with teddy bears while he was asleep.

For a time, Louis and Harry rented a £3m London apartment previously owned by footballer Ashley Cole. They threw a New Year's Eve party at what they describe as their 'pimped-out penthouse' and Louis hired a coach to bring 50 of his school friends down from Yorkshire for the wild bash.

'Every now and then, I get this urge to do some daft stuff. It all started with me trying to throw an apple core into the bin, which somehow turned into everyone picking up any fruit they could find. For those five minutes, it was so much fun!'

Louis Tomlinson

'They're all *awesomely*

talented guys, stupidly

good-looking, of course.

They've got everything, they've

got the *whole package*.'

Tom Fletcher, McFly

Up All Night

One Direction's debut album – *Up All Night* – was
released in the UK in November 2011 and four months
later in the States, featuring 13 songs that the boys
co-wrote with a series of top producers who had worked
with Lady Gaga, Beyoncé and Britney Spears. They began
work as soon as they had finished filming *The X Factor*,
once Simon Cowell had signed them to Syco Music. Being
runners-up on the show proved no barrier to success
and the catchy first single from the album, 'What Makes
You Beautiful', sold more than 100,000 copies in its first
weekend and topped the iTunes chart within 13 minutes
of being released.

The fastest-selling album of the year, it debuted at No. 2 in
the UK and was only kept off the top spot by Rihanna's *Talk
That Talk*. It went on to top the charts in Australia, Croatia,
Italy, Mexico, New Zealand and Sweden, reaching the Top
10 in a total of 20 countries. The hysteria surrounding their
first release led to comparisons with Westlife and Take That,
who the boys all idolize.

The Songs

Up All Night opens with the up-tempo lead single, 'What
Makes You Beautiful', and is followed by 'Gotta Be You' – a
rock ballad that became the band's second single. The third

song, 'One Thing', was described by Syco Music as 'an epic pop smash-in-waiting, featuring soaring vocal harmonies, powerhouse guitar riffs and an anthemic chorus that refuses to leave your head.' Niall and Liam have said it's their favourite track on the album.

The fourth song, 'More Than This', is a slow ballad, and Harry's favourite. After that comes party anthem 'Up All Night', which namechecks one of the boys' favourite artists, Katy Perry. The sixth cut is 'I Wish', followed by 'Tell Me A Lie' – originally intended for Kelly Clarkson, who later said: 'I loved that they liked it – they sound really great on it.' After that comes 'Taken', then 'I Want', which was written by Tom Fletcher from McFly. The album finishes with 'Everything About You', 'Same Mistakes' and 'Save You Tonight'.

Critical Reaction

As well as the fans loving it, *Up All Night* also went down a storm with music critics, who raved about its anthemic pop songs and youthful lyrics about having fun and heartbreak. Allmusic's Matthew Chisling described *Up All Night* as a 'classic boy band album', adding that 'One Direction is perfectly positioned to take the world by storm'. Digital Spy's critic Robert Copsey called it 'an adorable as expected debut, with a surprising amount of bite,' while the *Daily Star* awarded it eight out of 10, saying that 'the lads' big personalities shine through on its belting fun pop anthems.

The boys were thrilled when 'What Makes You Beautiful' won the BRIT Award for Best British Single at the 2012 ceremony at London's O2 Arena, although in the excitement Harry accidentally thanked Radio 1 instead of Capital Radio, whose listeners had voted for the winner, and their music was briefly banned from the station. The band-mates also forgot to thank their parents, but that did not stop the boys from celebrating the huge popularity of their song.

The first three singles taken from *Up All Night* went straight into the UK Top 10 and 'What Makes You Beautiful' became the most pre-ordered single in Sony Music Entertainment history. It also topped the charts in Australia and New Zealand, the Flemish Ultratop 50 and the Canadian Hot 100.

The Tour

In September 2011, to coincide with the eighth series of *The X Factor*, the team at Syco came up with a clever way to hook young fans: they had to complete a challenge on the official One Direction website to unlock the album title and cover, which showed the band members on the beach.

When they announced 24 tour dates, the tickets sold out within minutes. The shows kicked off in Watford on 18 December 2011, ending in Belfast a month later. Then it was announced that there would be an Oceania leg of the tour, with dates across Australia and New Zealand set for April 2012, followed by 27 dates in America.

'We've got some great songs on the album, which show off all our voices.'

Louis Tomlinson

Take Me Home

In November 2012, a year after the UK release of *Up All Night*, the boys were thrilled to bring out *Take Me Home*. Recorded in Stockholm, the album went straight to No. 1 in more than 30 countries, selling over 1 million copies in the first week. It was quickly praised by critics, many of whom singled out Niall's guitar playing. They became the first boy band in US chart history to achieve two No. 1 albums in one calendar year.

The title of the new album was 'leaked' by Louis in August when he included the hashtag #takemehome in one of his tweets. Fans, predictably, went bonkers, retweeting #takemehome every few seconds.

'Everyone's said that second albums are the hardest, so before we started recording we were a bit nervous.'

Harry Styles

'We always want to push for as much writing as possible because we want it to sound as real and as genuine as possible. It's really important for us to be part of that writing process. We hope to do more with every album.'

Louis Tomlinson

Living It Up

'Live While You're Young' was the eagerly anticipated first single from the boys' new album. Released in September 2012, the song was a top 5 hit around the world. Written by same trio of Rami Yacoub, Carl Falk and Savan Kotecha who had penned One Direction's first hits, 'What Makes You Beautiful' and 'One Thing', the single was not without its critics, many of whom claimed that it lifted a riff from the intro of The Clash's 'Should I Stay Or Should I Go?'.

The video for the song was filmed at a 'secret place' in Kent, UK, and featured the quintet camping, playing football and generally frolicking around at a pool party with a giant microphone and an inflatable banana. Needless to say, upon official release, the clip was viewed 8.24 million times in just 24 hours, breaking the previous record set by Justin Bieber's 'Boyfriend' of 8 million views in 24 hours.

A Good Thing

'Little Things', an Ed Sheeran penned heart-tugger, was released in the UK at the same time as the album, making the boys the first band to land a No. 1 in both the single and album charts at the same time. The song is accompanied by acoustic guitar, which, in the video, is provided by a confident Niall. They even played it to the Queen, at the 2012 Royal Variety Performance.

> *'As soon as we started recording music, we were aware that people would be surprised by it because it's not typical boy-band music. There's nothing else out there like our sound at the moment, it's completely new – it's One Direction's sound and we love it!'*
>
> Zayn Malik

Friends and Collaborators

Although their new album featured many veteran songwriters and producers, the boys were very proud of the fact that they co-wrote many of the tracks. The song, 'Back For You' was particularly poignant for Louis, who said that it was 'the one we wrote the majority of the lyrics for... It's all about being away on tour and missing our girlfriends.' The boys particularly enjoyed working with Ed Sheeran, with whom they not only recorded songs, but, according to Niall, had watermelon fights.

> *'We miss home a lot, but we love being on the road.'* Niall Horan

McFly's Guys

Another of pop's most successful songwriters, Tom Fletcher of McFly, was also on hand to help the famous five out with a track on *Take Me Home*. Having penned 'I Want' for the boys' debut album, they were chuffed to bits when he agreed to collaborate with them again. Before writing the song, they hung out with Tom and fellow McFly-er Danny Jones, sparking up the barbecue, chilling and generally having 'a fun time', according to Louis. The result was the uptempo 'I Would', noted by one critic as 'one of *Take Me Home*'s best surprises'. A big fan of McFly, Louis also admitted that the guys act as role models to him and his fellow band members, saying 'They've been so successful because they've managed to be themselves from the start. There aren't any egos.'. Wise words indeed.

Here's Looking At You

Being catapulted from total obscurity into a world of superstardom where their every move is watched, discussed and analysed by armies of adoring fans has proved an overwhelming experience for Harry, Zayn, Liam, Niall and Louis. Although some moments are pretty hair-raising, especially when mobbed by huge crowds, the boys are slowly starting to get used to the glare of the spotlight. The first time they flew into Heathrow Airport together after *The X Factor*, they were stunned by the enormous throng of girls waiting for them.

The Entourage

Harry admits it can be a struggle keeping his feet on the ground when surrounded by an entourage of staff, ready to cater to the boys' every whim. They are also getting used to being told what to wear by their stylist Caroline Watson. 'The boys are all quite individual in their styles,' she says. 'I've tried to carve out an identity in their style for them, which they all love and are really growing into.' Hairdresser Lou Teasdale is always at hand to make sure the band-mates are perfectly groomed, while celebrity bodyguard Jacquie Davies watches their backs. She said: 'It would have been so easy for them to go down the spoilt brat route, having found fame so young, but they are the complete opposite – lovely, polite boys, who are an absolute pleasure to work with.'

'There was literally a wall of fans. I got hit in the face by mistake in the scuffle and some of the other lads had clothes ripped off. Someone had hold of my hood, so I ended up being squashed up against the side of the van – it was all quite dramatic.'

Liam Payne, after being mobbed by fans

'I'm trying my best to stay as down-to-earth as possible so I don't want people doing things for me that I could do myself. I'm capable of picking up my own water, so why should they have to do it?' Harry Styles

The Image

While millions of girls want to be with them, just as many boys want to look like One Direction and high streets everywhere are now full of copycat fashions. The first trend they sparked was quirky jumpsuits after they were spotted in *The X Factor* house wearing distinctive all-in-ones from Norwegian label OnePiece – Jump In. So many people wanted to get their hands on one that the Oslo-based designers sold out in days. It has also been good news for Toms, makers of the eco-friendly shoes that Louis always wears, and sales of the Fred Perry tennis trainers Niall prefers have also surged. After Harry was spotted in the front row of the Aquascutum catwalk show at London Fashion Week, the classic British label became cool all over again, in the process giving Harry a whole new set of fans.

'I want to sit on Harry Styles' lap! I have a total crush on him. He walked past me at the Aquascutum show and I was salivating; I like his curly hair and he looks like a little cherub.'

It-girl Poppy Delevigne

The Bodies

Since their fans like almost nothing better than when the boys reveal an inch or two of naked flesh, the band-mates have to make sure they are honed and toned to perfection. That means hours spent working out in the gym, whether they like it or not.

Liam is by far the most enthusiastic trainer and uses protein powder to bulk up, but the group are all kept in shape with tough dance routines choreographed in the UK by *The X Factor*'s Brian Friedman and, when in America, they work with Britney Spears' ex-boyfriend, creative director and choreographer Wade Robson. But when it comes to getting the boys to stick to a healthy diet, the team have their work cut out – they all love pizza and Nandos' chicken, while Louis' favourite food is a bacon, egg and cheese sandwich dipped in brown sauce!

'I ask Niall if he wants to go to the gym and he says, "I'll see you there," then never turns up – unless he's hiding under the weight bench, lifting 40 kg and I didn't spot him!'

Liam Payne

> *'We've met some amazing children through working with Rays of Sunshine and feel honoured to be in a position to help. The charity gives thousands of seriously ill kids the chance to take time out and have some fun, and we are delighted to help wherever we can.'*
>
> *Zayn Malik*

We Love You

It should come as no great surprise that the boys have some very famous fans, including America's First Lady, Michelle Obama, who is so smitten that she invited them to the annual Easter Egg Hunt at the White House, held on Easter Monday 2012. Unfortunately, their hectic promotional schedule did not allow the visit, but they cheekily asked if they could come back another time. They have also caught the eye of Arnold Schwarzenegger's daughter Katherine, though Harry is perhaps understandably wary of the *Terminator* star!

British recording artist Lily Allen tweeted her congratulations to the boys on their success and they also proved a hit with the notorious Kardashians. In March 2012, Niall tweeted Khloe, inviting her to attend a concert for 7,000 fans in Dallas, and just a few weeks later, Harry made a shameless attempt to grab her sister Kim's attention by turning up to a radio interview in the States, holding a massive poster of her in a bikini with a Post-It note attached, saying: 'Call me, maybe?' It sounds unlikely, but the same technique worked for him when he wooed his ex-girlfriend Caroline Flack in shamelessly posing with a sign that read: 'To Flackster! Never too old. Let's make it happen!! Lots of love, Harry S'.

> *'Imagine having Arnie as your dad-in-law!' Harry Styles*

Popularity Contest

Since Harry is easily the most adored band member in the UK and has more Twitter followers than the others, the plan was to make him the lead singer as most boy bands in the States have a recognized frontman. Initially, he was given leading roles, however across the Atlantic, Niall has found himself more popular than the others. US fans seem to love his All-American looks, so much so that Simon Cowell banned him from dyeing his blond hair. Although pursued by excited admirers wherever he goes, Niall insists he is not much of a ladies' man, but that has not stopped American singer-songwriter and actress Demi Lovato from declaring her affection: 'He's so adorable!' she said. When quizzed on a possible romance, Mr Horan admitted: 'I'd like to see her all right and she's a similar age.'

Charity Work

The boys may now be superstars, but they're not letting all the attention go to their heads and still insist on helping others as much as they can. In fact, they interrupted their world tour to pay a visit to cancer-stricken schoolgirl Niamh Power in May 2012. The eight-year-old was delighted at the surprise visit arranged through charity Rays of Sunshine. One Direction are ambassadors for the organization, which grants wishes for seriously ill children between 3 and 18 years old; they often visit patients at home, and invite special fans backstage

'I would like to carry on what we're doing and get bigger, better and stronger. I want to go everywhere and do everything!'

Niall Horan

'I've not actually been on too many dates. I just like sitting at home, chilling and watching a movie.'

Niall Horan

before and after their shows in the UK. They also joined forces with JLS to record a single, a cover of Rose Royce's 'Wishing On A Star', for the children's charity Together For Short Lives, and in October 2011 Zayn posed topless to help raise funds for Teenage Cancer Trust.

The Doubters

It's almost impossible to imagine anyone not liking the adorable quintet, but the boys have managed to make one or two enemies along the way. Indeed, they are currently being sued by an American group, who claims they owned the name first. In April 2012, the US One Direction filed a lawsuit, asking for a court order to force the British band to change its name. In the legal documents, the American band (also made up of five cute boys) says it formed in 2009, a year before Niall, Zayn, Liam, Harry and Louis had even met. Although they have a much lower profile, the group – who say they filed a trademark application first – is also suing Syco and Sony Music for £1m in damages, according to papers filed in California Central District Court.

'One Direction's management tried to resolve the situation amicably when the matter first came to light,' explained a spokesman for the British boys. 'One Direction's lawyers now have no choice but to defend the lawsuit and the band's right to use their name.'

'As a band, we're having the absolute best time ever. We've become better friends than I could ever have imagined and it's so nice to have four other lads to share this experience with. I think we're going to get tighter and tighter as time goes on.'

Harry Styles

The Directioners

Dedicated fans are known as 'Directioners' and they are so devoted to the boys' happiness that one girl from Boston was distraught when it rained in her hometown during the band's visit – in case it meant they would never come back! 'One Direction are in my city,' said Megan Connor, 'which means that I am breathing the same air as them.'

With girls permanently camped outside their homes and hotels, it seems they are living every teenage boy's dream; Harry admits that it can be a struggle not to let all the adoration go to their heads. 'We get a lot of praise,' he says. 'Obviously it's lovely to hear and it always puts a smile on your face but I want to keep my feet on the ground as much as possible.'

Dealing With the Fans

For such young lads, One Direction have shown surprising maturity when it comes to dealing with the lavish attention they receive from exceptionally eager fans. Despite girls throwing themselves at Harry, Niall, Zayn, Liam and Louis, they are careful who they choose to hang out with and make sure they are not caught in compromising positions with girls they barely know.

'We have the most unbelievable fans,' says Niall. 'When we were staying in a hotel in Richmond, girls were outside in

'We have had to use the hotel service lift. There are girls in the main lift the whole day, just going up and down, hoping to bump into us!'

Harry Styles

'It can be strange – waking up to people screaming at 7am – but we love it!'

Liam Payne

sleeping bags or booking into rooms on the same floor as us. And every day after school, there would be about 400 or 500 fans there.'

In France, soldiers were called in to clear an exit route for the band as they attempted to board the Eurostar train at Gare du Nord, and in LA, where the boys bagged their own TV show on the Nickelodeon channel, they were forced to use back doors and secret entrances.

The Presents

The boys are constantly lavished with gifts, including carrots and cereal (*see also* page 18)! Ever since Louis once joked that he loves girls who like carrots, he has been inundated with carrot banners, T-shirts and, of course, real vegetables. And while Liam receives licorice, Harry gets olives (as an ironic joke, even though he hates them) and one fan actually presented the group with portraits of their faces painted on Portobello mushrooms!

Jealous Frenzies

After Harry hooked up with presenter Caroline Flack during their stint on *The X Factor* and the couple were spotted on a date at London's St Martin's Lane Hotel in November 2011,

she was besieged with online abuse and received a slew of death threats. However, Harry inflamed the situation still further: when asked which of the contestants was his favourite, he referred to the 15-year age gap between himself and Caroline, saying: 'They're all a bit young for me.' Caroline was said to be terrified by the abuse and it only stopped when they split up in January 2012.

Emma Ostilly, another of Harry's former flames, also became a target for bitter fans after she started dating the star, and had to close down her Twitter account after receiving online abuse.

Liam's now ex-girlfriend, dancer Danielle Peazer, also endured death threats and name calling from jealous fans, but did little to stop the nasty bullying when she tweeted a photo of herself sunbathing in LA with a topless Liam by her side, in a move which inevitably made his fans green with envy.

Hi One Direction fans! To clarify. I'm close friends with Harry. He's one of the nicest people I know. I don't deserve death threats:) x

Caroline Flack, via Twitter, November 2011

'One night, two girls dressed as carrots were dancing at the bottom of the stage – it was brilliant and I love all that. Mind you, I should probably be getting some kind of cut from farmers, because I'm sure carrot sales must have gone up!'

Louis Tomlinson

Out And About

As they continue to top the charts and conquer hearts around the world, Harry, Liam, Zayn, Niall and Louis are busier than ever. Barely out of their teens, the boys have hectic daily schedules packed with sell-out concerts, TV performances and endless personal appearances. There is even a movie in the pipeline and they have taken America by storm, scooping three MTV Video Music Awards along the way.

Olympic Gold

The roar of the crowd was deafening as One Direction entered the Olympic Stadium on the back of a lorry to perform at the closing ceremony of London 2012. With a global audience of over one billion people, they knew the eyes of the entire world were on them as they played their biggest ever gig.

Continuing their quest for worldwide domination, the fabulous five sang their hearts out on the night but it was Zayn who stole the show by unveiling a blonde quiff under a cool fedora hat; within moments, talk of his new hairstyle was trending on Twitter! Despite the huge scale of the event, the boys appeared unfazed as they belted out their hit 'What Makes You Beautiful', following performances by pop veterans that included The Spice Girls, Madness and Pet Shop Boys. Although the boys were still showbiz newcomers compared to some of the acts that took to the stage in August 2012, critics agreed they appeared just as confident as stars more than twice their age.

'For me the Olympics literally can't be topped. Just the feeling of being in that room, all our families were there. The whole feeling was just unbelievable.'

Harry Styles

Rock Royalty

At the Royal Variety Performance in November 2012, the Queen applauded as the boys sang 'Little Things', which was No. 1 at the time of the high-profile show. Afterwards they had the huge honour of being introduced to Her Majesty the Queen, and mingled with the stars backstage at the Royal Albert Hall in London. They all agreed it was most definitely a career highlight, but just weeks later they confirmed their status as the biggest boy band on the planet by selling out Madison Square Garden.

Their performance at New York's famous stadium won rave reviews from American music critics who declared there was something special about One Direction – although their voices were almost drowned out by the screams of 20,000 fans at the concert. The 90-minute show, which was opened by Ed Sheeran, was seen as a prelude to One Direction's fan convention in New Jersey the next day, where fans from more than 35 countries around the world were flown in as part of a Golden Ticket package.

Afterwards, Harry was spotted holding hands with American country singer Taylor Swift, sparking rumours about a romance and causing Taylor to be likened to Yoko Ono, who was famously blamed for splitting up The Beatles. Their romance fizzled out within weeks, however, and following the prestigious gig, One Direction's album *Take Me Home* reached the top of the charts in the US.

'*I don't **ever want** this to **end**, really. I don't **think** it needs to as **long** as we **keep doing** what we're doing and **making** the **right music**.*'

*Liam Payne,
on 1D's mega-success*

Waxing Lyrical

In April 2013, One Direction were immortalised in wax after the famous waxwork museum Madame Tussauds was overwhelmed by requests to feature the boys. The five lifelike models, which cost £150,000 each to create, were then taken on a global tour, beginning in London, before travelling to New York, and then onto Sydney, where they were proudly displayed to satisfy the demands of their devoted fans.

Each of the boys had two sittings for the model-makers, where hundreds of measurements were taken to ensure the waxworks were as lifelike as possible. When the figures were finally unveiled, eager fans queued for hours to pose with their idols' wax twins and of course hundreds of girls insisted on kissing and squeezing the statues. Two days before the exhibition opened to the public, the band met their life-size counterparts at a secret meeting and were all thrilled by the uncanny resemblances.

'*All the **biggest stars** around the world get these **wax figures** made of them and why are we, **five** normal **lads**, getting these made? It's an amazing honour, really cool.*'

Zayn Malik

Sing Out

Although they had smashed the charts all over the world by the start of 2013, the boys were determined to continue with their run of success and kept a stream of chart hits coming.

On Tour

Before their 2012 tour was even over, the boys announced plans for another one, to start in February 2013. Selling out in minutes, extra dates were added to an already gruelling schedule between February and October. Their 2013 Take Me Home world tour involved a total of 117 shows in Europe, Australasia and America. And to top it all, the boys no longer had to behave like mere mortals and queue at airports, but were instead whisked between venues in their very own luxury private jet, dubbed Air Force One Direction.

Ticket sales reached a staggering 300,000 within a day of being released in the UK and Ireland – including seats for a six-date sell-out at London's O2 Arena. In Australia and New Zealand, the boys sold out all 18 shows – selling 190,000 tickets within hours.

On their first visit to the States, they needed 20 bodyguards each for their first 45-minute performance in Dallas, and when they returned in May 2013 they were protected from

> *'"Kiss You" holds a special place in our heart, and it kind of sets the tone … for the album. There were proper sets and everything for this video, and there was a lot of hard work that went into it with the crew and everything.'*
>
> *Liam Payne*

their obsessive fans by highly trained secret service agents and ex-Marines who once ensured the safety of US President Barack Obama. Luckily they appeared to love the attention, and always remembered to thank their devoted fans for their support.

Kiss You

The boys proved – as if we didn't already know it – that they know how to keep their fans happy when they stripped down to their swimming trunks for the video of 'Kiss You'. They cleverly recreated a series of scenes inspired by classic films and bands from the Fifties and Sixties, but it was their tribute to The Beach Boys that caused the most excitement. As the boys bared their chests while pretending to surf, Harry had a rare flash of shyness and actually covered his nipples! They also recreated scenes from Elvis Presley's 'Jailhouse Rock' and an iconic image of The Beatles from their 1964 hit 'A Hard Day's Night', but the song only reached No. 9 in the UK chart.

Harry paid tribute to another of their songs from *Take Me Home* by adding the words 'Little Things' to his tattoo collection. The nod to their No.1 single pushed Harry's collection of body art to well over 30 tattoos, which includes swallows, his sister's name written in Hebrew, cities his band has performed in, crucifixes and 17Black, James Bond's lucky gambling number.

One Way Or Another

Their next release, a charity single to raise funds for Comic Relief, was a bigger success, and stormed into the British charts at No. 1. To film the official video for the special mash-up of Blondie's 'One Way Or Another' and The Undertones' 'Teenage Kicks', the boys were invited to meet the British Prime Minister at Downing Street. David Cameron said he enjoyed his brief role alongside the lads, adding 'Glad to help with the filming location!' It has become a tradition for Prime Ministers to send themselves up for Comic Relief: in 2007 Tony Blair starred alongside Catherine Tate in a special sketch, and in 2011, after losing the General Election, Gordon Brown appeared with JLS and James Cordon.

As part of their fundraising efforts, One Direction also flew to Ghana with Comic Relief, but meeting children in the Agbogbloshie slum in the capital Accra left them all close to tears. The moving footage, which was broadcast during the charity's bi-annual telethon, led to a massive spike in donations.

The band also performed the No. 1 song at the 2013 Brit Awards, where they had another triumphant night and took home the newly created Global Success Award.

'It kind of put things into perspective for me … in everyday life you have little problems that we think are so major, and then you go over there and you see people that are actually dealing with real problems.'

Zayn Malik

'We want to bring out a record nearly every year, every year and a half.' Niall Horan

> '*The worst thing a guy could do for a girl? Personally I think it's to ignore her while she's loving you with all her heart.*'
>
> *Liam Payne*

Up Close And Personal

Although the boys seem to be a close-knit and wholesome bunch, they are careful not to appear too squeaky clean, and they all have fun in their private lives, too.

Too Many Broken Hearts?

When Liam split from girlfriend Danielle Peazer in 2013, his fans may have been delighted but his personal security was immediately stepped up as it was felt that hopeful girls would target him more than ever. Meanwhile, Niall's romance with MTV presenter Laura Whitmore was swiftly denied after she reunited with her ex-boyfriend, and Harry proved he was still available when he kissed as many fans as he could when the band were mobbed on arrival in Paris in April 2013. However, he found himself having to defend his close friendship with Radio 1 DJ Nick Grimshaw, who said their shared sense of humour made them best friends despite the ten-year age gap.

The long distances and time apart also took its toll on Zayn and his Little Mix girlfriend Perrie Edwards, who split briefly amid rumours he had cheated on her, but they were reunited within weeks.

The Talented Mr Styles

Harry remains the most popular member of the band, obsessed fans mob him every time he steps out in public – and he loves it! He usually poses for scores of photos with his

admirers and plants kisses on as many girls as he can. Ten French policemen were called in to protect him as he landed at Charles de Gaulle airport in Paris in April 2013, and in Oslo he reportedly hooked up with 18 year-old student Camilla Foss after being invited onto a bus for a party. As he left his £1,400 a night hotel in Sweden in May – during their massive 2013 World Tour – a girl managed to sneak past his team of burly bodyguards and grabbed him.

His fans are certainly a passionate bunch, and tend to turn against any woman connected with Harry. Singer Taylor Swift received death threats when she dated him briefly at the end of 2012. It did not help that she wrote a song about him called 'I Knew You Were Trouble', and Harry described dating her as 'a pain in the arse'.

When his bodyguard's niece Fia Litton posted pictures of herself with Harry she was also subjected to a barrage of abuse. More recently he was linked to model Cara Delevingne and Rod Stewart's daughter Kimberley after they were spotted on a date in LA. She is 14 years older than Harry, who has a reputation for preferring older women.

'A dream is only a dream, until you decide to make it real.'

Harry Styles

Fly On The Wall

British TV station Channel 4 is set to release a movie about the boys, but their documentary film will focus on the fans, celebrating the Directioners die-hard devotion through social media. The programme will look at how the most dedicated fans interact with the band using different types of online media. The one-off Cutting Edge special called *I Heart One Direction* aims to get under the skin of the most passionate fans to find out what it really means to be a Directioner.

Executive producer Tayte Simpson said: 'It will offer a fascinating insight into a new breed of idol worship. Social media has created huge communities which connect millions of fans in a way that was never possible before. One Direction's use of social media to diarise their inner thoughts gives fans a sense of intimacy and ownership, fuelling strong emotions.' Will Bloomfield, the group's manager, said: 'These guys live online, and so do their fans.'

'We've been *writing* and *recording* it [the new album] while on *tour*. We are *really happy* with it. We don't want to *rush* it but it *will be* out for *Christmas*.'
Louis Tomlinson

'Every *now* and *then* you have like a *realization* moment where you get *goosebumps* and think: I am *literally* the *luckiest* person in the *world*.' Niall Horan

All About Us

Since fans are desperate for an insight into any and every aspect of their idols' lives, the band have allowed some of their most intimate moments to be recorded in a film called *One Direction: This Is Us*. The movie gives a rare glimpse of what the boys got up to behind the scenes on their recent tour. The feature-length film, directed by acclaimed documentary filmmaker and Academy Award nominee Morgan Spurlock, is guaranteed to be a hit.

Boys On Film

Shot over many months, *This Is Us* is part documentary, part 3D concert movie, telling the story of how 1D were created by Simon Cowell on *The X Factor*, and following their meteoric rise as they break different countries, including America and Japan. Simon described the decision to hire Morgan Spurlock, who is famous for his documentary *Supersize Me*, as very cool, adding: 'I think it's going to be amazing. Spurlock was such a fan of doing it.'

Spurlock was given unprecedented access to every aspect of their lives, and even tweeted a picture of a sleepy looking Harry in bed, which of course sparked a frenzy of excitement. The hotly anticipated film also shows their families and features interviews with the boys describing their dreams and what their phenomenal rise to fame actually feels like.

They return to their hometowns for the film, with Harry visiting the bakery in Cheshire where he used to work at the age of 14. Although they are no longer together, Liam's ex-girlfriend Danielle agreed that footage of them as a couple could stay in the movie, set for release in August 2013, as they remain close friends. Harry, however, insisted that all footage of his former flame Taylor Swift be cut from the final edit.

Boy Power

The boys have a knack for creating a frenzy of excitement around themselves, mostly thanks to their constant online activity. Their management employs a social media team and the members all tweet messages and photos themselves, several times a day.

Their busy website is updated constantly, so there was widespread hysteria when they unveiled the poster for the film, which features thousands of photos sent in by fans from around the globe. Fans can zoom in on the mosaic of tiny photos to see if they are part of the picture, or search for locations where they may have been spotted. The poster also 'comes to life' when a Zapcode is scanned with a smartphone, unlocking exclusive video content of the band.

There seems to be nowhere the most powerful band on the planet can be left in peace – after becoming the first British group to ever enter the US Billboard chart at No. 1 with their debut album they became superstars in the States. In Norway there is even a radio station dedicated purely to the boys. P41D plays only One Direction songs!

'There comes a day when you realize turning the page is the best feeling in the world, because you realize there's so much more to the book than the page you were stuck on.'

Zayn Malik

'I haven't *met a girl* yet *who* I'd want to *even* think of getting *serious* with. I think I've been *unlucky* in *love* so far. I'm longing to *meet someone* who really *inspires me* and makes me *really* want to *spend* time with *them*.'

Harry Styles

One Big Announcement

The boys kept their army of fans on tenterhooks in May 2013 as their website ticked down to a mysterious announcement. Speculation was rife, with rumours that the band was unveiling a new member, a musical or even giving fans a chance to star in their movie. When the news finally broke that the boys would be embarking on another world tour in 2014, the site crashed due to the millions of Directioners desperate for details.

The Where We Are Tour sees the boys taking to the biggest stadiums around the world. They will head to Latin America in April 2014 for gigs across the continent including Peru, Chile and Brazil before returning home for massive shows closer to home in Sunderland's Stadium of Light, the Etihad Stadium in Manchester and Dublin's Croke Park, and will end the tour after two months on the road with further gigs in Edinburgh and Wembley Stadium – where they made the announcement.

Although many fans were disappointed the tour would not take the boys back to the States, they added to the frenzy of excitement by promising to add more concerts, including dates in Spain, Italy and Japan. Louis also talked about their new album, also called *Where We Are*, which has 'a rockier and edgier tone to it', to be released by the end of 2013. It is predicted this will earn the boys a staggering £50 million between them.

'We don't *mind* having *haters*. As *long* as we have our *girls*, we are *strong*.' Zayn Malik

ISBN 978-1-907424-15-1

Dymuna'r cyhoeddwr
gydnabod cymorth
Cyngor Llyfrau Cymru.

Cyhoeddwyd gan Wasg y Bwthyn, Caernarfon.
Argraffwyd gan Wasg Gomer.

PEN LLŶN HARRI PARRI

LLUNIAU: MIKE HARRISON

The World At Their Feet

One Direction have defied even their fiercest critics and achieved what many assumed would be impossible: they have cracked not just America but Canada and Australia as well. Over the years, scores of boy bands have dreamt of making it big around the world, and record labels have invested vast fortunes in trying to promote their groups, including Take That and Duran Duran, but since The Beatles, few British boy bands have actually managed to achieve this. The lads are understandably proud because they have worked so hard to achieve their burning ambitions.

'My hopes for the future? To take over the world! You've got to aim high.' Louis Tomlinson

Going Global

These days, nothing the boys do is on a local scale. When they released their first DVD *Up All Night – The Live Tour* in May 2012, they sent legions of fans into a frenzy by organizing a worldwide viewing party; the boys announced precisely when they would be watching the footage and tweeting along, while fans were encouraged to watch at home at the same time. As the band-mates revealed all kinds of gossip and

insider info from the show, they rewarded their favourite tweeters with follows and retweets. Needless to say, the ambitious plan was a huge success and several more similar interactive projects are in the pipeline.

Something Special

As if appearing in a 3D movie on our big screens isn't enough, the boys are set to invade our living rooms once again! With their third studio album due out in time for Christmas 2013, the boys will be caught up in a promotional whirlwind. Insiders at ITV have revealed that producers at the channel are in talks with the boys' management about filming an hour-long special featuring several of their new tracks. The audience for the show – which is tipped for a prime time slot straight after *The X Factor* final – will be made up of fans and their famous friends.

Making Millions

They may be millionaires and in demand all over the world, but the boys are determined to keep their feet on the ground, no matter how famous they become. Although they have played in front of packed stadiums and Queen Elizabeth II, and appeared at the London 2012 Olympics Closing Ceremony, the lads credit their tight-knit families and close friends with making sure they do not let the adoration go to their heads. Thanks to that, One Direction may well take over the world, and we can be sure they will do it with cheeky grins on their faces. We can't wait!

'My main aim for us in the long term is to be big in America – that's my ultimate dream. It's going to take a lot of work, but we're all really determined. This is our chance to have an amazing time, doing what we love to do and we're not going to let that pass us by for anything.'

Liam Payne

FURTHER INFORMATION

ONE DIRECTION INFO

NIALL

Birth Name:	Niall James Horan
Birth Date:	13 September 1993
Birth Place:	Mullingar, County Westmeath, Ireland
Height:	1.71 m (5 ft 7 in)
Star Sign:	Virgo

ZAYN

Birth Name:	Zayn Javadd Malik
Birth Date:	12 January 1993
Birth Place:	Bradford, England
Height:	1.75 m (5 ft 9 in)
Star Sign:	Capricorn

LIAM

Birth Name:	Liam James Payne
Birth Date:	29 August 1993
Birth Place:	Wolverhampton, England
Height:	1.77 m (5 ft 10 in)
Star Sign:	Virgo

HARRY

Birth Name:	Harry Edward Styles
Birth Date:	1 February 1994
Birth Place:	Holmes Chapel, Cheshire, England
Height:	1.77 m (5 ft 10 in)
Star Sign:	Aquarius

LOUIS

Birth Name:	Louis William Tomlinson
Birth Date:	24 December 1991
Birth Place:	Doncaster, South Yorkshire, England
Height:	1.75 m (5 ft 9 in)
Star Sign:	Capricorn

DISCOGRAPHY

Albums

Up All Night (2011)

Take Me Home (2012)

Singles

2010: 'Heroes' (as *X Factor* 2010 finalists; UK No. 1)

2011: 'What Makes You Beautiful' (UK No. 1; US No. 4)

'Gotta Be You' (UK No. 3)

'Wishing On A Star'

(with *The X Factor* 2011 finalists; UK No. 1)

2012: 'One Thing' (UK No. 9)

'More Than This'

'Live While You're Young' (UK & US No. 3)

'Little Things' (UK No. 1)

2013: 'Kiss You'

'One Way Or Another (Teenage Kicks)' (UK No. 1)

TOURS

Up All Night Tour (2011–12)

Take Me Home Tour (2013)

Where We Are Tour (2014)

AWARDS *(INCLUDING)*:

BBC Radio 1 Teen Awards

2012: Best British Album (*Up All Night*)

Best British Single ('One Thing')

Best British Music Act

Billboard Music Awards

2013: Top New Artist

Top Duo/Group

Top Pop Artist

BRIT Awards

2012: Best British Single ('What Makes You Beautiful')

2013: BRITs Global Success

MTV Awards

2012: Best New Act (EMAs)

Best UK & Ireland Act (EMAs)

Biggest Fans (EMAs)

Best New Artist (VMAs)

Best Pop Video (VMAs)

Most Share-Worthy Video (VMAs)

Nickelodeon Kids' Choice Awards

2012: Favourite UK Newcomer (UK)

Favourite UK Band (UK)

2013: Favourite UK Band (UK)

Favorite Music Group (US)

Favorite Song ('What Makes You Beautiful') (US)

People's Choice Awards

2013: Favorite Album (*Up All Night*)

Favourite Song ('What Makes You Beautiful')

Teen Choice Awards

2012: Choice Music: Breakout Group

Choice Summer Music Star: Group

Choice Music: Love Song ('What Makes You Beautiful')

ONLINE

onedirectionmusic.com:

Official site in many languages, with news, photos, events and store

myspace.com/onedirection:

Check this site out for One Direction's latest songs and videos

facebook.com/onedirectionmusic:

Find out what 1D are up to

twitter.com/onedirection:

Share your thoughts with the 1D boys and other Directioners @onedirection

raysofsunshine.org.uk:

Charity granting wishes to seriously ill children aged 3–18

BIOGRAPHIES

Nadia Cohen

Nadia Cohen is an entertainment journalist who has worked at a number of national newspapers and magazines, including *Grazia* and the *Daily Mail*. As a showbusiness correspondent, she covered film festivals, premieres and award ceremonies around the world. Nadia was headhunted for the launch of a new American magazine, *In Touch Weekly*, and spent several years living and working in New York. *In Touch* now has a readership of over a million, while Nadia lives in London and juggles family life with showbiz news and gossip. Previous titles for Flame Tree include *Justin Bieber: Oh Boy!*.

Mango Saul

Mango Saul has been a music, lifestyle and entertainment journalist for ten years. Some of his highlights include having breakfast at Waffle House with rapper Ludacris in Atlanta, sharing a bed with Destiny's Child for a *Smash Hits* cover interview and being sent an ice-cream costume for no reason. As editor of Sugarscape.com, Mango has seen the site grow to over 4 million page views per month and was shortlisted for Digital Editorial Individual 2011 at the AOP Awards.

PICTURE CREDITS

All images © Getty Images:

Don Arnold/WireImage: 56, 93; Neilson Barnard: 10, 16, 72, 100, 112, 114; Tony Barson/WireImage: 142; Dave M. Benett: 134; Gareth Cattermole: 94; Lester Cohen/WireImage: 132; D. Dipasupil/FilmMagic: 69; Stephen M. Dowell/Orlando Sentinel/MCT: 109; FOX: 129, 140, 149, 150; Jon Furniss/WireImage: 8; Ian Gavan: 22; Gary Gershoff/WireImage: 60; Marc Grimwade/WireImage: 36, 160; Dave Hogan: 14; Mark Holloway/Redferns: 66, 155; Hagen Hopkins: 20, 29, 106; Samir Hussein/Redferns: 138; Chris Hyde: 49; Matt Kent: 7; Kevin Kane: 1 (top right); Michael Kovac/WireImage: 25, 30, 43, 156, 159; Jeff Kravitz/FilmMagic: 38; Jason LaVeris/FilmMagic: 1 (centre), 125, 131; Scott Legato: 40; Stephen Lovekin: 70, 105, 116; Steve Mack/FilmMagic: 26; Mike Marsland/WireImage: 146; Danny Martindale: 118; Kevin Mazur: 137; Kevin Mazur/WireImage: 59, 152; Marty Melville/AFP: 64, 96; Jeff J. Mitchell: 126; Michelle Moore/WireImage: 13; Chiaki Nozu/WireImage: 102; Joseph Okpako/FilmMagic: 34, 84; Al Pereira/WireImage: 53, 77; Ryan Pierse: 88, 90, 98; George Pimentel/WireImage for MuchMusic: 86; Christopher Polk: 62, 121; Debra L; Rothenberg/FilmMagic: 82; Jun Sato/WireImage: 122; Ilya S. Savenok: 50, 74; Lawrence Smith/Fairfax Media via Getty Images: 44, 78; Myrna Suarez: 1 (bottom right), 4; Kenzo Tribouillard/AFP: 1 (top left); Venturelli: 19; Slaven Vlasic: 46, 54; Tim Whitby: 145; Kevin Winter: 110; Paul Zimmerman/WireImage: 81